Reading Skills
1-2

Written by
Beth Barber

D1514975

Editor: Carla Hamaguchi
Illustrator: Darcy Tom
Designer/Production: Moonhee Pak/Carmela Murray
Cover Designer: Barbara Peterson
Art Director: Tom Cochrane
Project Director: Carolea Williams

Table of Contents

Introduction

Each book in the *Power Practice*™ series contains over 100 ready-to-use activity pages to provide students with skill practice. The fun activities can be used to supplement and enhance what you are teaching in your classroom. Give an activity page to students as independent class work, or send the pages home as homework to reinforce skills taught in class. An answer key is included at the end of each book for verification of student responses.

The practical and creative activities in the reading skills books provide the perfect practice with over 20 reading skills. Each book is divided into sections covering these various skills.

Reading Skills 1–2 provides activities that will directly assist students in practicing and reinforcing skills such as
• beginning and ending sounds
• word families
• drawing conclusions
• context clues
• categorizing events and ideas
• following directions
• sequencing
• predicting
• analogies
• main idea and details

Use these ready-to-go activities to "recharge" skill review and give students the power to succeed!

Starting Sounds

Beginning Sounds

Consonant blends are two or three consonants that are blended together to create a sound.

Look at each picture. Use a blend from the box to complete each word. Practice reading all the words when you are finished.

br	cl	sk	sl	st	sn

_____ ide

_____ ore

_____own

_____ ail

_____ y

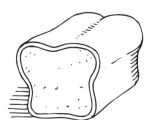

_____ ead

_____ ick

_____ unk

_____ oud

Can you think of another word that begins with any of the consonant blends in the box?

Consonant Blend Tally

Beginning Sounds

Read each word. Listen for the beginning consonant blend. Circle it. Put a tally mark next to the consonant blend you hear in each word.

crow	grab	bleed	floor
proud	train	please	black
crab	trick	grown	flower
trade	play	glad	blast
fly	plow	great	trot
blue	trap		

Consonant Blend	Tally	Total
cr		
gr		
bl		
fl		
pr		
tr		
pl		
gl		

Which blend had the most tally marks? _____

The Blend That Does Not Belong

Beginning Sounds

Say the beginning blend for each picture. Draw a rectangle around the word that does **not** begin with the same beginning blend as the picture.

1   smile   smoke   smart   drip

2   swam   clutter   sweet   swat

3   clap   frill   clip   clock

4   free   from   fry   smell

5   dress   dragon   drop   sweater

Write the words that have a rectangle around them.

1 _____

2 _____

3 _____

4 _____

5 _____

Find the Blend

Beginning Sounds

Beginning Consonant Blends							
tw	sk	st	sp	fr	gr	gl	wh

Read the rhymes. Underline all of the words that begin with a consonant blend. Write the words you underlined. If the word appears more than one time, only write it once.

Twinkle, Twinkle Little Star
Twinkle, twinkle little star,
How I wonder where you are.
Up above the world so high
like a diamond in the sky.
Twinkle, twinkle little star,
How I wonder where you are.

❶ _____

❷ _____

❸ _____

❹ _____

❶ _____

❷ _____

❸ _____

❹ _____

❺ _____

Five Little Speckled Frogs
Five little speckled frogs
Sat on a speckled log
Eating a most delicious bug.
Yum! Yum!
One jumped into the pool
Where it was nice and cool.
Now there are four green speckled frogs.
Glub! Glub!

Reading Skills • 1–2 © 2004 Creative Teaching Press

Name _____

Fill in the Blend

Beginning Sounds

Use a word from the box to complete each sentence.

broom	crib	dress	fruit	crab
princess	frost	drum	blanket	bring

1 I will _____ you your breakfast.

2 Use the _____ to sweep the floor.

3 A baby sleeps in a _____.

4 The _____ married the prince.

5 A _____ will keep you warm.

6 Your _____ is very pretty.

7 Beat on the _____.

8 There is _____ on the window from the cold night.

9 A _____ walked out of the water.

10 An apple is a kind of _____.

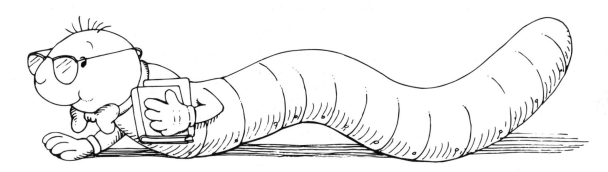

X Marks the Sound

Medial Sounds

Read each word. Listen carefully to the sound in the middle of the word. All of the words have a long vowel sound in the middle. Complete the chart by drawing an X in a box next to the sound you hear in each word.

fuse	mule	line	rice
late	fire	face	table
seal	gate	feed	wave
team	game	sneeze	green
boat	comb	coat	home
tone	phone	cake	night

Long Vowels

/a/																	
/e/																	
/i/																	
/o/																	
/u/																	

Which long vowel sound did you hear the most? _____

Reading Skills • 1–2 © 2004 Creative Teaching Press

Word Change

Medial Sounds

When you change the vowel in the middle of a word, you create a whole new word. Use the vowels **a, i,** and **o** to fill in the blanks for each row of words. Practice reading the words. Then circle the "nonsense" word and write it on the line below.

t____p   t____p   t____p

h____t   h____t   h____t

r____ck   r____ck   r____ck

p____t   p____t   p____t

bl____ck   bl____ck   bl____ck

_____ is a nonsense word.

Now pick two words from above and use each in a sentence.

_____

_____

_____

_____

Sound Bubble

Medial Sounds

Read each word. Fill in the bubble next to the sound you hear in the middle of each word.

bowl	**mule**	**lake**
○ a ○ e	○ a ○ e	○ a ○ e
○ i ○ o	○ i ○ o	○ i ○ o
○ u	○ u	○ u

nine	**dish**	**hot**
○ a ○ e	○ a ○ e	○ a ○ e
○ i ○ o	○ i ○ o	○ i ○ o
○ u	○ u	○ u

green	**bat**	**bug**
○ a ○ e	○ a ○ e	○ a ○ e
○ i ○ o	○ i ○ o	○ i ○ o
○ u	○ u	○ u

pen
○ a   ○ e
○ i   ○ o
○ u

Reading Skills • 1–2 © 2004 Creative Teaching Press

Missing Middle

Medial Sounds

Look at each picture. Use a middle sound from the box to complete each word.

oo	ou	ea	oa

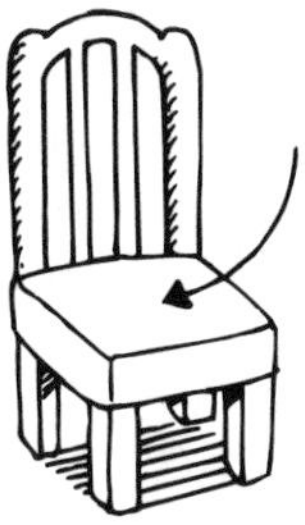

l____f

g____t

s____t

c____t

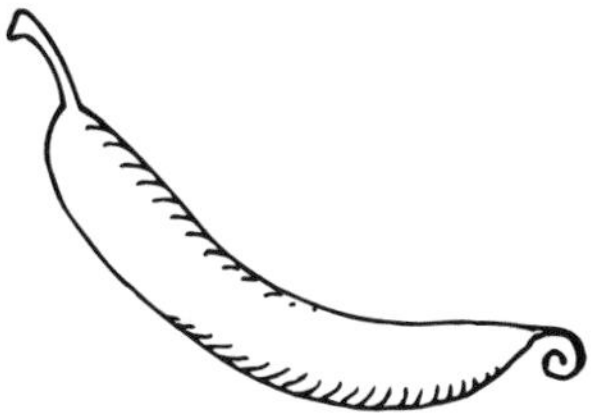

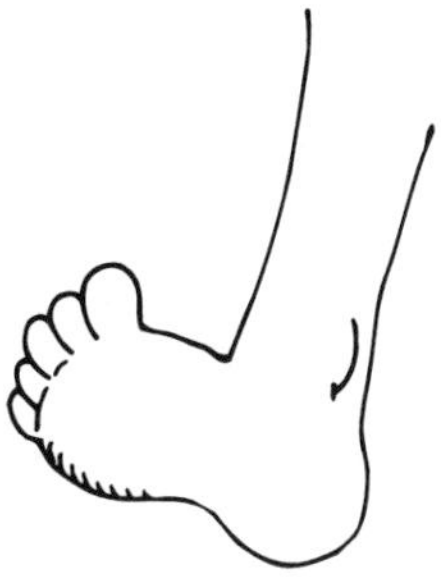

b____n

f____t

m____se

sp____l

m____n

h____se

h____d

t____m

Short Seesaw Sounds

Medial Sounds

Read each word in the box. Decide which short vowel sound you hear in the middle of the word. Write each word on the matching seesaw.

bat	cup	fish	hen	not
pin	lap	met	pop	fun

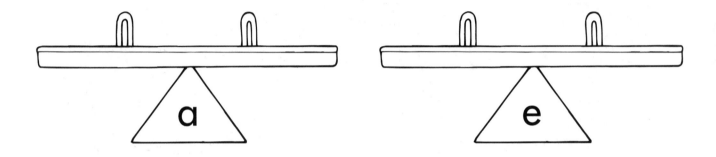

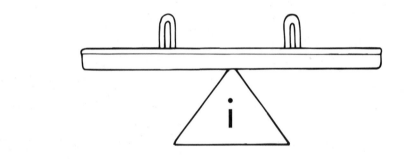

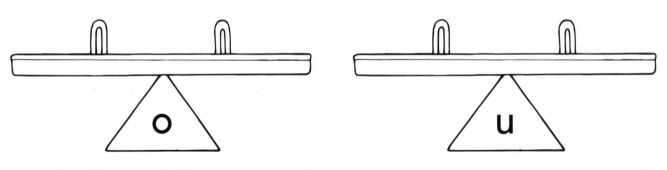

Reading Skills • 1–2 © 2004 Creative Teaching Press

Watermelon Words

Ending Sounds

Read the word on each seed. Write a word that has the same ending sound on the watermelon.

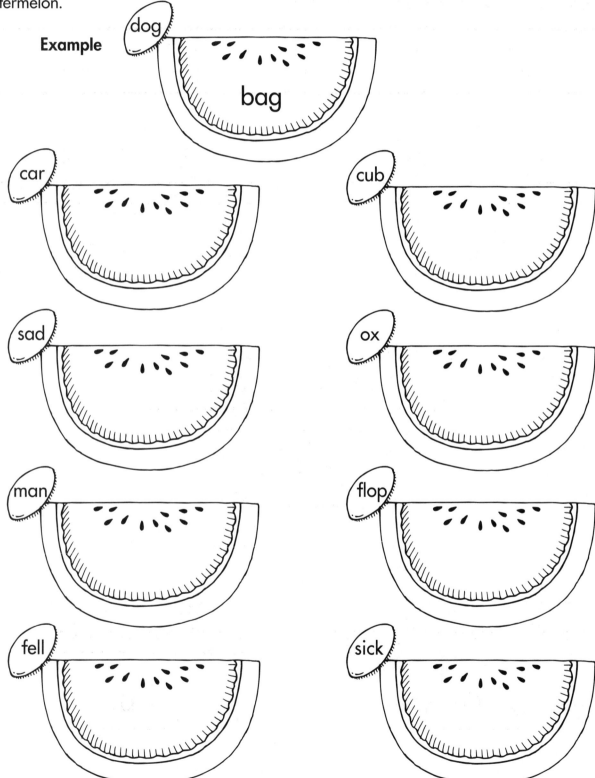

Example

dog

bag

car

cub

sad

ox

man

flop

fell

sick

It's a Match

Ending Sounds

Read the words in the box. Listen for the ending sound. Write each word under the sound you hear at the end of the word.

game	kitty	daddy	hole
sky	stole	dime	butterfly

m

_____

_____

e

_____

_____

l

_____

_____

i

_____

_____

Reading Skills • 1–2 © 2004 Creative Teaching Press

Finish the Word

Ending Sounds

Say the name of each picture. Write the ending sound that is missing in each word.

fo_____

pai_____

kin_____

mo_____

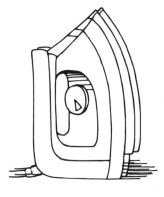

iro_____

des_____

pape_____

ghos_____

han_____

Name _____

Circle the Sound

Ending Sounds

Say the name of each picture. Circle the ending sound.

f   v   k

k   t   x

p   d   t

n   f   g

sh   ch   s

x   k   r

k   ch   t

n   p   h

t   d   k

Reading Skills • 1–2 © 2004 Creative Teaching Press

Ending Sound Bubble

Ending Sounds

Say each word. Fill in the bubble next to the sound you hear at the end of the word. Pay careful attention. The ending letter is not always the same as the ending sound!

candy		
○ e		○ m
○ n		○ i
○ a		○ d

dumb		
○ a		○ e
○ i		○ d
○ n		○ m

phone		
○ a		○ e
○ n		○ d
○ u		○ i

my		
○ a		○ e
○ i		○ d
○ u		○ r

ride		
○ a		○ e
○ i		○ d
○ u		○ o

they		
○ a		○ e
○ m		○ d
○ u		○ t

play		
○ a		○ e
○ m		○ d
○ u		○ l

Rhyme in a Line

Rhyming Words

Read each set of rhyming words. Use a rhyming word from the box to complete each set.

heat	net	dock	must	hand	sun
found	line	bake	catch	hike	flight

1. fun, stun, _____

2. stand, band, _____

3. fine, mine, _____

4. jet, set, _____

5. sock, lock, _____

6. match, latch, _____

7. sound, hound, _____

8. just, trust, _____

9. bike, like, _____

10. treat, seat, _____

11. cake, rake, _____

12. night, right, _____

Rhyming Clues

Rhyming Words

Read each clue. Find the rhyming word from the box that matches the clue and write it on the line.

look	sit	cake	feet	jug	light
broom	bird	door	hair	tooth	had

1 Rhymes with **book** _____

2 Rhymes with **bear** _____

3 Rhymes with **booth** _____

4 Rhymes with **store** _____

5 Rhymes with **night** _____

6 Rhymes with **mug** _____

7 Rhymes with **meat** _____

8 Rhymes with **sad** _____

9 Rhymes with **make** _____

10 Rhymes with **lit** _____

11 Rhymes with **heard** _____

12 Rhymes with **room** _____

Bubble Time Rhyme

Rhyming Words

Read each set of words. Fill in the bubble next to the word that does not rhyme with the other words in the box.

○ small	○ book	○ treat	○ chair
○ fall	○ bat	○ meat	○ bear
○ tall	○ look	○ tree	○ hair
○ smell	○ hook	○ seat	○ cheek
○ door	○ bag	○ ant	○ snug
○ desk	○ flag	○ apple	○ bug
○ core	○ sag	○ pant	○ snail
○ floor	○ bee	○ rant	○ rug
○ hall	○ twig		
○ doll	○ big		
○ mall	○ tan		
○ had	○ fig		

Reading Skills • 1–2 © 2004 Creative Teaching Press

Nursery Time Rhymes

Rhyming Words

Read the nursery rhymes. Pay close attention to the underlined words. For each underlined word, find a rhyming word and draw a circle around it.

Jack and <u>Jill</u> went up the hill
To fetch a pail of water;
Jack fell <u>down</u> and broke his crown
And Jill came tumbling after.

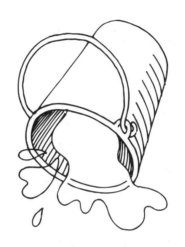

Hey, diddle <u>diddle</u>!
The cat and the fiddle,
The cow jumped over the <u>moon</u>.
The little dog laughed
To see such sport
And the dish ran away
With the spoon.

Little Jack <u>Horner</u>
Sat in the corner
Eating his Christmas <u>pie</u>.
He stuck in his <u>thumb</u>,
And pulled out a plumb
And said, "What a good boy am I."

Rhyme Time

Rhyming Words

Read each clue. Write the correct rhyming word.

1 It begins with /h/ and rhymes with **and**.

What is the word? _____

2 It begins with /b/ and rhymes with **hand**.

What is the word? _____

3 It begins with /st/ and rhymes with **band**.

What is the word? _____

4 It begins with /l/ and rhymes with **stand**.

What is the word? _____

5 It begins with /s/ and rhymes with **land**.

What is the word? _____

6 It begins with /str/ and rhymes with **sand**.

What is the word? _____

Reading Skills • 1–2 © 2004 Creative Teaching Press

Name _____

Sight Word Search

Sight Words

You hear sight words when talking and see them in almost everything you read. Read the sight words in the box. Then read the advertisements below. Circle the sight words in each advertisement.

out	eight	some	only	seven
walk	who	once	pull	could
four	want	two	very	come

Lost
Four kittens lost
eight pairs
of mittens.
Call at once
if found.

Found
Some very sweet
seven-week-old
puppies.
I had to pull them
out of a box.

Wanted
A babysitter
who could walk
to my house
two days a week.

Car for Sale
Do you want a
good car for
only a small price?
Come see me at
once.

Name _____

Fill in the Sight Word

Sight Words

Use a sight word from the box to complete each sentence.

wrote	climb	from	you	do	again
have	eyes	eight	half	said	your

1 Pick up _____ clothes.

2 _____ not cross the street alone.

3 The milk is _____ gone.

4 The number _____ comes after seven.

5 I _____ you a letter.

6 We _____ to take a bath.

7 Do not do that _____.

8 "Go to bed," _____ Dad.

9 I love _____.

10 I got the vase _____ the store.

11 _____ the tree.

12 You have pretty blue _____.

Reading Skills • 1–2 © 2004 Creative Teaching Press

See the Sight Words

Sight Words

Review the list of sight words in the chart. Look for these words as you read the story. Circle them. Then put a tally mark in the chart for each time you circled the word in the story.

Once upon a time there were three billy goats. The billy goats were hungry because there was not enough food where they lived. The goats often thought if only they could cross the bridge to the other side, there would be plenty of grass to eat on the hillsides. Then they could eat and eat and never be hungry.

But there was a problem. Under the bridge there was a troll who wanted to eat anyone who went across the bridge. The billy goats were so hungry they decided to forget about the troll and cross the bridge. "Who is that crossing over my bridge?" yelled the troll.

"Oh, it is only I, the smallest billy goat, going to the hillside to make myself fat."

"No, you are not. I am going to climb onto the bridge and eat you up at once!" said the troll.

only	once	were	was	to	you

Which word did you find the most often? _____

Reading Skills • 1–2 © 2004 Creative Teaching Press

Name _____

 # Sight Word Study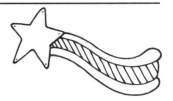

Sight Words

Write each sight word in the correct column. Some words can be placed in more than one column.

are	again	come	do	eyes	for	from	have
one	other	pull	of	said	they	was	you

3-Letter Sight Words	4-Letter Sight Words
Words That Begin with a Vowel	**Words That End with a Vowel**

Reading Skills • 1–2 © 2004 Creative Teaching Press

Common Sight Words

Sight Words

Use a sight word from the box to label each picture.

eyes	eight	water	climb	four
seven	half	two	one	

_____

_____

_____

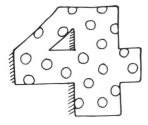
_____

_____

_____

_____

_____

_____

Name _____

 # Combine the Compound

Compound Words

A **compound word** is two words put together to form a new word.
Example: birth + day = birthday

Draw a line from a word in the first column to a word in the second column to create a compound word. Write each compound word.

Compound Word

base	room	_____
cup	work	_____
class	plane	_____
home	pen	_____
star	cake	_____
sail	ball	_____
air	fish	_____
out	bath	_____
back	bird	_____
bird	boat	_____
blue	side	_____
play	pack	_____

Reading Skills • 1–2 © 2004 Creative Teaching Press

Can You Find the Compounds?

Compound Words

Read the story. Underline the compound words. (Some words are used more than once.)
Then write each compound word once on the lines below.

Once upon a time there was a grandmother who liked to
help her grandson with his homework. They used newspaper,
a paintbrush, and a notebook to complete the homework.
Then, they each ate a blueberry muffin, a cupcake, and some
popcorn. The next day, the grandson put his homework in his
backpack and took it to his classroom.

1 _____

2 _____

3 _____

4 _____

5 _____

6 _____

7 _____

8 _____

9 _____

10 _____

11 _____

Name _____

 # Compound Clues

Compound Words

Read the clues. Write the correct compound word from the box for each clue.

paintbrush	snowstorm	doghouse	sailboat
backpack	mailbox	homework	snowman
raincoat	basketball	newspaper	popcorn

1 Schoolwork to be done at home _____

2 A brush used to paint _____

3 Corn that pops _____

4 A boat that sails _____

5 A paper you read that tells about the news _____

6 A ball that you shoot in a basket _____

7 A man made out of snow _____

8 A pack that you wear on your back _____

9 A coat that you wear in the rain _____

10 A house where a dog sleeps _____

11 A storm of snow _____

12 The box that holds mail _____

Reading Skills • 1–2 © 2004 Creative Teaching Press

Compound Crossword

Compound Words

Combine each pair of words to form a compound word. Use the compound words to complete the puzzle.

Across
1. ant + hill = _____
2. horse + fly = _____
4. star + fish = _____
6. tea + pot = _____
7. play + pen = _____

Down
1. air + plane = _____
3. light + house = _____
5. base + ball = _____

Name _____

Fill in the Compound

Compound Words

Use a compound word from the box to complete each sentence.

sunshine	campground	football	birthday
inside	firefighter	rainbow	afternoon
swimsuit	barnyard	anyone	outside

1 We will go to the park later in the _____.

2 The _____ feels warm.

3 Tomorrow is my _____ party.

4 Let's go play _____.

5 Throw the _____ to me!

6 Put on a _____ so we can go to the pool.

7 There are horses and cows in the _____.

8 Can _____ hear me?

9 The brave _____ put out the flames.

10 Look at all of the colors in the _____.

11 We will put up the tent at the _____.

12 We must play _____ because it is raining.

Reading Skills • 1–2 © 2004 Creative Teaching Press

Word Family Bubble

Word Families

Read each set of words. Fill in the bubble next to the word that does **not** belong to the word family.

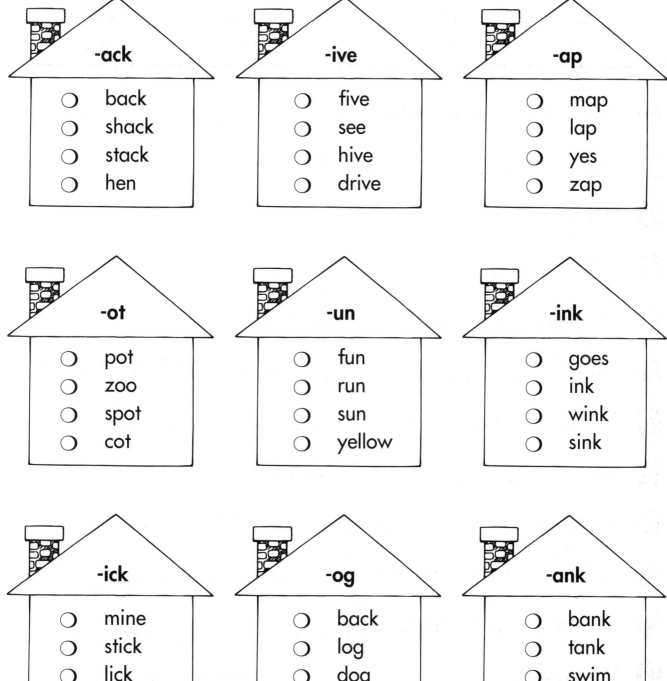

-ack
- ○ back
- ○ shack
- ○ stack
- ○ hen

-ive
- ○ five
- ○ see
- ○ hive
- ○ drive

-ap
- ○ map
- ○ lap
- ○ yes
- ○ zap

-ot
- ○ pot
- ○ zoo
- ○ spot
- ○ cot

-un
- ○ fun
- ○ run
- ○ sun
- ○ yellow

-ink
- ○ goes
- ○ ink
- ○ wink
- ○ sink

-ick
- ○ mine
- ○ stick
- ○ lick
- ○ trick

-og
- ○ back
- ○ log
- ○ dog
- ○ frog

-ank
- ○ bank
- ○ tank
- ○ swim
- ○ thank

Finish the Family

Word Families

Read the words in each word family. Fill in the missing part on the final word.

came
blame
fame
g_____

shut
hut
rut
n_____

fate
gate
date
sk_____

dose
nose
hose
r_____

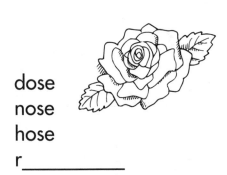

coat
goat
float
b_____

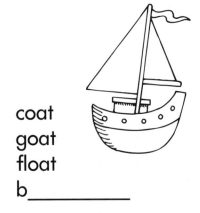

tock
lock
rock
s_____

hum
glum
sum
g_____

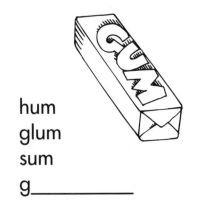

fell
sell
tell
b_____

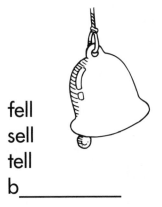

nice
rice
mice
d_____

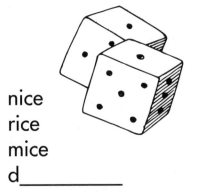

Reading Skills • 1–2 © 2004 Creative Teaching Press

Name _____

Form a Family

Word Families

Read each word. Place it in the house with the matching word family. Some word families may have more words than others.

mole	mail	jet	rain	met	grain	truck
rig	hit	van	lit	hill	sail	gain
stuck	will	buck	fill	pan	sole	pig
ran	big	fail	pet	brain	let	rail
bit	hole	whole	bill	fan	duck	spit

-ain

-ail

-ole

-uck

-an

-ill

-it

-ig

-et

Reading Skills • 1–2 © 2004 Creative Teaching Press

Name _____

Family Riddles (-ug)

Word Families

Form a word family by changing the beginning sound or sounds in a word and keeping the ending the same.

Follow the directions to form each new word for the word family.

1 The word is **rug**.
Change the /r/ to /b/.
What is the new word?

_____

4 The word is **lug**.
Change the /l/ to /h/.
What is the new word?

_____

2 The word is **bug**.
Change the /b/ to /t/.
What is the new word?

_____

5 The word is **hug**.
Change the /h/ to /d/.
What is the new word?

_____

3 The word is **tug**.
Change the /t/ to /l/.
What is the new word?

_____

6 The word is **dug**.
Change the /d/ to /j/.
What is the new word?

_____

Write two words that would belong in a word family with the word **jet**.

_____   _____

Reading Skills • 1–2 © 2004 Creative Teaching Press

Family Riddles (-ain)

Word Families

Form a word family by changing the beginning sound or sounds in a word and keeping the ending the same.

Follow the directions to form each new word for the word family.

1 The word is **train**.
Change the /**tr**/ to /**ch**/.
What is the new word?

_____

4 The word is **gain**.
Change the /**g**/ to /**p**/.
What is the new word?

_____

2 The word is **chain**.
Change the /**ch**/ to /**m**/.
What is the new word?

_____

5 The word is **pain**.
Change the /**p**/ to /**r**/.
What is the new word?

_____

3 The word is **main**.
Change the /**m**/ to /**g**/.
What is the new word?

_____

6 The word is **rain**.
Change the /**r**/ to /**sp**/.
What is the new word?

_____

Write two words that would belong in a word family with **bath**.

_____   _____

Name _____

Make It Make Sense

Words with Multiple Meanings

Many words have more than one meaning. Reading a sentence carefully can help you understand the correct meaning of a word.

Use a word from the box to complete each sentence. You will use each word two times, but the meaning will change.

duck	fall	sink	pen	note	shake

1 Let's _____ hands.

2 You should _____ under a table if there is an earthquake.

3 If there is too much water in the boat, it will _____.

4 Be careful not to _____ off your bike.

5 Look at the _____ swimming in the pond.

6 A pig lives in a _____.

7 Ask a parent to write a _____ if you are absent.

8 During the _____ season, trees have few leaves.

9 Wash your hands at the _____.

10 Use a _____ to write your name.

11 Please take _____ of the new due date.

12 She ordered a vanilla _____ to go with her burger and fries.

Reading Skills • 1–2 © 2004 Creative Teaching Press

Name _____

Which Meaning Makes Sense?

Words with Multiple Meanings

Read the underlined word in each sentence. Circle the definition that best fits the way the word is used in the sentence.

1 | Please <u>set</u> the table.

to put dishes on the table
a group of something

4 | The child sat in her mother's <u>lap</u>.

upper part of the legs when sitting
to go around or back and forth

2 | The gift is in the <u>box</u>.

a container that holds something
a kind of fighting

5 | Be careful not to <u>slip</u>.

what you wear under a dress
to fall

3 | Please <u>rock</u> the baby to sleep.

a kind of stone
to sway back and forth

6 | Don't <u>ram</u> into the car.

a kind of animal
to bump into something with force

Pick one of the underlined words and draw pictures to show its meanings.

word: _____

Reading Skills • 1–2 © 2004 Creative Teaching Press

Name _____

Multiple Meaning Crossword Puzzle

Words with Multiple Meanings

Read each clue. Find the word from the box that matches the clue. Use your answers to complete the puzzle.

pit	bed	band	back
pick	pants	shine	

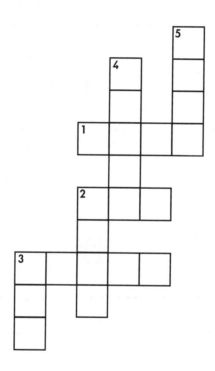

Across
1. A tool or when your mom says "_____ up your toys"
2. Where you plant flowers or where you sleep
3. Something you wear or what a dog does after it runs a lot

Down
2. A group that plays music or a piece of elastic that holds things together
3. A hole or a seed
4. What the sun can do or cleaning your shoe
5. A part of your body or a direction

Reading Skills • 1–2 © 2004 Creative Teaching Press

Multiple Meaning Sentences

Words with Multiple Meanings

Write a sentence for each picture to show how a word can have more than one meaning.

seal

1 _____

2 _____

spring

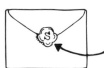

1 _____

2 _____

shake

1 _____

2 _____

Name _____

Multiple Meaning Clues

Words with Multiple Meanings

Look at each pair of pictures. Write one word that describes both pictures.

1 The word that describes both pictures is _____.

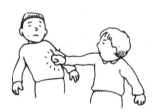 

2 The word that describes both pictures is _____.

3 The word that describes both pictures is _____.

4 The word that describes both pictures is _____.

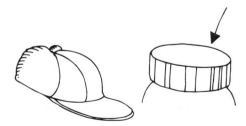

5 The word that describes both pictures is _____.

tick
tick
tick

Reading Skills • 1–2 © 2004 Creative Teaching Press

Similar Synonyms

Synonyms and Antonyms

Words that have similar meanings are called **synonyms**.
Example: *small* and *tiny*

Read the words in the chart. Write two synonyms for each word in the chart. Use the words in the box to help you.

build	chilly	carton	container	little	create
cold	kind	yell	weep	shout	tiny
giant	sob	large	pleasant		

small	scream	big	nice
_____	_____	_____	_____
_____	_____	_____	_____

make	box	cool	cry
_____	_____	_____	_____
_____	_____	_____	_____

Name _____

Synonym Balls

Synonyms and Antonyms

Read the pair of words inside each ball. Color the ball if the two words are synonyms.

said
told

sweet
sour

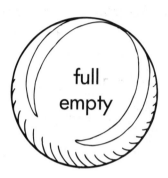
full
empty

cap
hat

rain
sun

jog
run

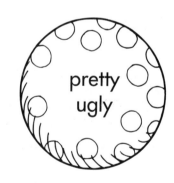
pretty
ugly

pal
friend

gift
present

finish
end

Antonym Seesaws

Synonyms and Antonyms

Words that have opposite meanings are called **antonyms**.
Example: *dark* and *light*

Read the pair of words on each seesaw. Color the seesaw if the words are antonyms.

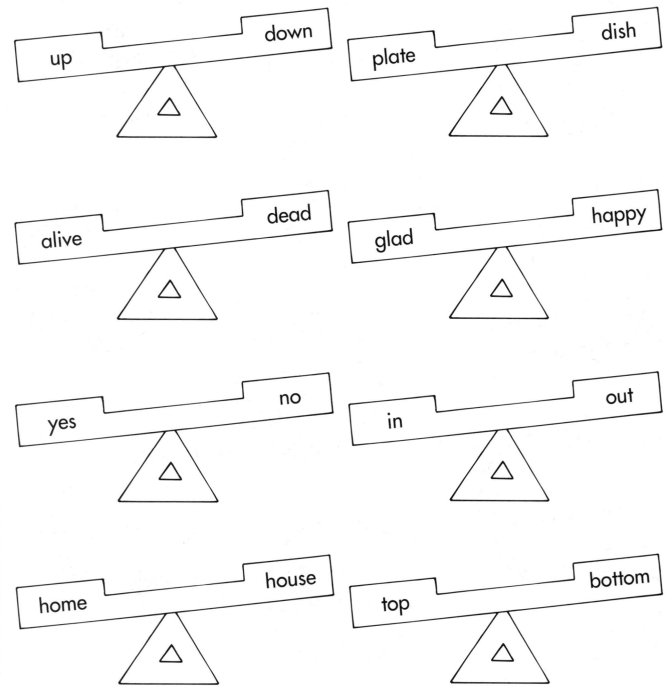

Name _____

Fill in the Antonym

Synonyms and Antonyms

Read each sentence. Complete the sentence by writing an antonym for the word below the blank. Use the words in the box to help you.

shut	old	thick	no	tall
awake	brother	off	sad	hot

1 _____ the door.
   open

6 The pants are _____.
   new

2 The soup is _____.
   cold

7 I feel _____.
   happy

3 The baby is _____.
   asleep

8 This is my _____.
   sister

4 She is _____.
   short

9 Dad said, "_____."
   yes

5 Turn the light _____.
   on

10 The book is _____.
   thin

48

Similar and Opposite

Synonyms and Antonyms

Read each word in the chart. List a synonym and an antonym for each word. Use the words in the box to help you.

nice	glad	small	dirty	bad	mean
sad	quick	big	country	cold	slow
city	frown	great	hot	grin	clean

Word	Synonym	Antonym
good		
town		
cool		
happy		
kind		
messy		
little		
fast		
smile		

Name _____

You Choose

Homophones

Homophones are words that sound alike but have different spellings and different meanings.
   Example: *buy, bye,* and *by*

Circle the homophone that correctly completes each sentence.

1 I _____ a sandwich for lunch. eight ate

2 My favorite _____ is a daisy. flour flower

3 She wore her _____ in braids. hair hare

4 My _____ and uncle went on vacation. aunt ant

5 My grandma _____ me a package. cent sent

6 _____ you have the time? Do Due

7 She _____ out her birthday candles. blue blew

8 I want to _____ the movie. see sea

9 Did you see the _____ in the forest? dear deer

10 He ate _____ pieces of pizza. two too

11 He was stung by a _____. bee be

12 Our team _____ the game. one won

Reading Skills • 1–2 © 2004 Creative Teaching Press

Name _____

Label It

Homophones

Write the homophone that correctly names each picture.

1  tail
tale

_____

2  tee
tea

_____

3  rows
rose

_____

4  clothes
close

_____

5  four
for

_____

6  son
sun

_____

Reading Skills • 1–2 © 2004 Creative Teaching Press

Fill in the Homophone

Homophones

Read the words in the box. Complete each sentence with the correct homophone.

buy	their	no	our	see
by	there	know	hour	sea

1 I saved my money so I could _____ a toy.

2 I did not _____ how to turn on the radio.

3 60 minutes equals one _____.

4 I wear glasses to help me _____ better.

5 _____ were many people at the zoo.

6 I want to sit _____ my mom.

7 There are many fish in the _____.

8 We think that _____ dog is cute.

9 Jim and Bill invited us to _____ house.

10 There was _____ way that she was going to eat bugs.

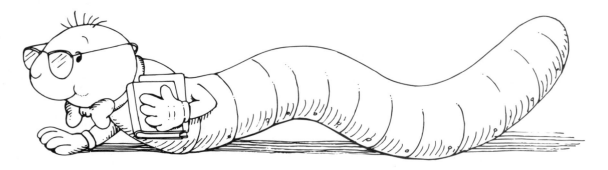

52

Homophone Search

Homophones

Homophones are words that sound alike but have different spellings and different meanings.
Examples: *two, too,* and *to*   *sun* and *son*
there, their, and *they're*   *so* and *sew*

Read the story. Circle the homophones.

The sun was shining brightly. It was a hot day, so Mary and Sue

decided to go to the beach. They called Mrs. Brown's son to see if he

wanted to go, too. He did, so the three kids rode their bikes to the beach.

It took them eight minutes to get there. They swam in the sea for two

hours. Then they went back home and ate lunch. They had so much fun

that they decided they would do it again next week.

Write the circled words. If a word is circled several times, just write it once.

_____   _____   _____

_____   _____   _____

_____   _____   _____

_____   _____   _____

_____   _____   _____

_____   _____

Name _____

Prefix Fill-In

Prefixes and Suffixes

Prefixes are letter groups added to the beginning of base words.

Prefix	Meaning	Example
mis-	poorly, not	misfit
un-	not	unmade
re-	again	recall
dis-	opposing	dislike
pre-	before	presoak

Read each sentence. Choose a word with a prefix from the balloons to complete each sentence.

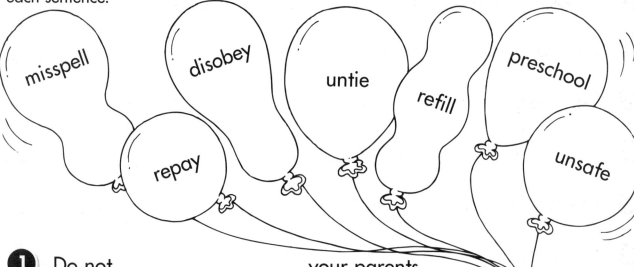

misspell disobey untie refill preschool repay unsafe

1 Do not _____ your parents.

2 Try not to _____ a word on the test.

3 It is _____ to climb that tree.

4 _____ your shoelace.

5 You must _____ the money.

6 My younger sister spends the morning in _____.

7 Please _____ my water glass.

Reading Skills • 1–2 © 2004 Creative Teaching Press

Prefix Production

Prefixes and Suffixes

Prefix	Meaning
mis-	poorly, not
un-	not
pre-	before
re-	again

Underline the word with a prefix in each sentence. Write the meaning of the word on the line.

1 Please refold your napkin. _____

2 The teacher will retell the story. _____

3 Don't forget to presoak the clothes. _____

4 Can you reread the poem? _____

5 The food was left uneaten. _____

6 I misunderstood the directions. _____

Add a prefix to each base word.

7 _____ call

8 _____ use

9 _____ handle

10 _____ told

11 _____ lucky

12 _____ view

13 _____ take

14 _____ finished

15 _____ move

16 _____ test

Name _____

Suffix Fill-In

Prefixes and Suffixes

Suffixes are letter groups added to the end of base words.

Suffix	Meaning	Example
-ful	full of	hopeful
-ly	in a way that is	happily
-less	without	helpless
-er	more	thinner

Read each sentence. Add a suffix from the balloons to the base word in each sentence.

1 It was pain_____ when I fell.

2 Please sit nice_____ on the floor.

3 The pen ran out of ink so it is use_____.

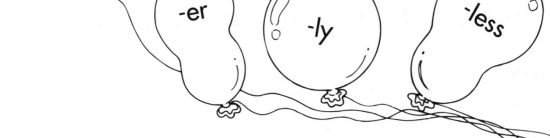

4 My cup is full_____ than yours.

5 The baby is help_____ without her mom or dad.

6 I would be happy_____ with ice cream than green beans.

7 I am power_____ and strong.

Suffix Sentences

Prefixes and Suffixes

Suffix	Meaning
-ful	full of
-ly	in a way that is
-less	without
-er	more

Underline the word with a suffix in each sentence. Write the meaning of the word on the line.

1 He talked loudly. _____

2 The man was helpful. _____

3 This paint is redder than I like. _____

4 You are acting foolishly. _____

5 The driver was fearless. _____

6 She always wears a cheerful smile. _____

Add a suffix to each base word.

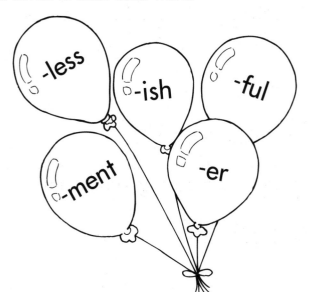

7 hope_____

8 strong_____

9 thought_____

10 child_____

11 agree_____

Name _____

Base Words

Prefixes and Suffixes

Read each word. Determine whether the word contains a prefix or a suffix and circle the correct choice. Then write the base word.

1 unfair   prefix   suffix   _____

2 likeable   prefix   suffix   _____

3 biggest   prefix   suffix   _____

4 happiness   prefix   suffix   _____

5 rename   prefix   suffix   _____

6 thickest   prefix   suffix   _____

7 childish   prefix   suffix   _____

8 cheerful   prefix   suffix   _____

9 misuse   prefix   suffix   _____

10 precut   prefix   suffix   _____

11 restart   prefix   suffix   _____

12 quickly   prefix   suffix   _____

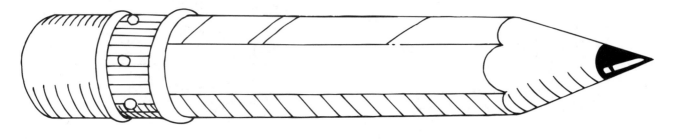

Reading Skills • 1–2 © 2004 Creative Teaching Press

Match the Contraction Pairs

Contractions

Contractions are a short way of writing two words. The apostrophe takes the place of a letter or letters.
  Example: *is + not = isn't*

Draw a line to match the two words in the first column with its contraction in the second column.

we are	won't
he is	you've
you are	isn't
we have	they've
she is	don't
they will	we're
will not	he's
they are	you're
do not	we've
you have	she's
is not	they'll
they have	they're

Name _____

Character Contractions

Contractions

Contractions are a short way of writing two words. The apostrophe takes the place of a letter or letters.
Example: "You're a beast!"   you are

Read each sentence. Underline the contraction. Then write the words that make up each contraction.

1 "Cinderella, you can't go to the ball." _____ _____

2 "Pinocchio, you aren't made out of wood anymore."

_____ _____

3 "Jack, he'll find you in the castle." _____ _____

4 "I'll huff and I'll puff and I'll blow your house in." _____ _____

5 "I'm coming up to eat you!" roared the troll. _____ _____

6 "She's sleeping in my bed," said the baby bear. _____ _____

7 "Who's the fairest of them all?" she asked the mirror.

_____ _____

8 "You've got to rescue Rapunzel." _____ _____

9 "Let's go to Neverland," said Peter Pan. _____ _____

10 "You'll behave as long as you're living under my ocean."

_____ _____   _____ _____

Reading Skills • 1–2 © 2004 Creative Teaching Press

Name _____

Contraction Choice

Contractions

Read each sentence. Circle the contraction that is made by the two underlined words.

1. You <u>do not</u> need to explain.   don't   didn't

2. I <u>was not</u> feeling well yesterday.   wasn't   hasn't

3. She <u>could not</u> go to the store.   shouldn't   couldn't

4. <u>We are</u> going to a movie.   We're   We'd

5. <u>They are</u> good friends.   They're   They've

6. <u>He is</u> fun to play with.   She's   He's

7. Mom <u>had not</u> gotten home from work.   hadn't   haven't

8. She <u>would not</u> eat the carrot.   wouldn't   won't

9. He <u>can not</u> go with us.   can't   couldn't

10. <u>She will</u> come to school tomorrow.   She's   She'll

11. <u>I have</u> been to Hawaii.   I'll   I've

12. I <u>will not</u> be at the party.   won't   wouldn't

Contraction Cross-Out

Contractions

Read the words in each box. Cross out the word that is **not** a contraction.

can't won't call	I I'm I'll	cold shouldn't couldn't
you'll will we'll	shirt she'll we'll	we've I've well
you're we're week	do doesn't didn't	ill It's I'm
like let's we've	aren't can't cold	he'd she'd they

Reading Skills • 1–2 © 2004 Creative Teaching Press

Name _____

Contraction Search

Contractions

Read the story. Underline the eleven contractions in the story.

Early one morning, Sam woke up and started scratching. "I can't take this itching. I'm going crazy!" Sam told his mom about the itching.

"You shouldn't keep scratching or you'll get scars. I'll have to call the doctor because she'll know what is the matter," explained Sam's mom. "Your doctor said that we've got to buy some special lotion for you and that you're to drink a lot of water and get some rest. It's certain that you have chicken pox! She doesn't want you scratching," Sam's mom said gently.

"I won't scratch," answered Sam.

1 Write the contractions that start with the letter **W**.

_____   _____

2 Write the two words for the contraction **can't**.

_____   _____

3 There are two contractions that always start with **I**. What are they?

_____   _____

4 Write the four contractions that end with **n't**.

_____   _____   _____   _____

Reading Skills • 1–2 © 2004 Creative Teaching Press

Prediction Practice

Making Predictions

When you are reading a story, it is exciting and helpful to guess what is going to happen next. This is called making a **prediction**.

Read each sentence. Circle the choice that shows what will probably happen next.

1 The vase is very close to the edge of the table.

The vase is going to fall.   A girl will fill the vase with flowers.

2 The little boy's eyes are closing and he is yawning.

He is going to fall asleep.   He is going to the movies.

3 The movie has a monster and the child is scared.

The child laughs.   The child cries.

4 The clouds are dark gray and the air is cold.

Children will go to the park and play.   It will rain.

5 The man is standing on the diving board near the pool.

He will dive into the pool.   He will put on a shirt.

6 The mommy bird has worms for the baby birds.

The baby birds will fly away.   The baby birds will eat.

7 A laughing girl is looking at beagle puppies through the window of a pet store.

She will walk away and not think of them again.

She will ask her parents if she can have a puppy.

Reading Skills • 1–2 © 2004 Creative Teaching Press

Sensible Predictions

Making Predictions

Read each statement and prediction. Color the cloud if the prediction makes sense.

The plant has no water or sunlight.
The plant will grow to be 3 feet tall.

The dog jumps up and down.
The dog will be taken for a walk.

The hungry baby has no teeth.
The baby's mother will give him soft food.

The student does poorly on the test.
The teacher will say, "Good job!"

The children sing happy birthday.
The birthday girl will blow out the candles.

The boy's family packs the car with a tent, sleeping bags, and bug spray.
They will go camping for the weekend.

It rains on the children.
The children will be dry.

The man does not like the food.
The man will eat all the food.

School Predictions

Making Predictions

Read the articles from the school newspaper. Write your prediction for each situation.

1 Four students were sent to the nurse with chicken pox on Thursday.

2 The school secretary reports that 60 students were absent yesterday.

3 The second grade class is going to the zoo on Monday. The weather forecast is for heavy rain.

4 The basketball team has won its last 20 games. The team plays again tonight.

1 _____

_____

2 _____

_____

3 _____

4 _____

_____

Name _____

Prediction Puzzlers

Making Predictions

Read each situation. Make a sensible prediction.

1 The student who most closely estimates the number of jelly beans in a jar wins the jar. It contains 50 jelly beans. Suzie guesses there are 40 jelly beans in the jar. Joe guesses there are 100 jelly beans in the jar. Whom do you predict will win the jar of jelly beans?

_____

2 The class made a "What is your favorite color?" graph. Each child could vote for red, yellow, or green. There were 2 votes for red. There were 17 votes for yellow. There was one vote for green. Which color do you predict the students wanted to paint the classroom?

_____

3 Walter goes to bed at 8:00 p.m. every night. He attended his grandpa's birthday party and went to bed at 10:00 p.m. on Thursday. Make a prediction about how Walter will feel on Friday morning. I predict Walter will feel

_____.

4 Kate has 3 hearts, 2 circles, 3 stars, and 2 squares. The teacher asks her to make a shape pattern on the table. Draw a sketch that shows the pattern Kate might make with these shapes.

Predicting Feelings

Making Predictions

Read each situation. Circle the word that describes how each person might feel.

1 John gets lost at Disneyland.
   happy   scared   tired

2 Freddy falls, breaks his arm, and misses his baseball game.
   surprised   good   sad

3 A broom unexpectedly falls out of the closet in front of Jenny.
   startled   angry   sleepy

4 On Saturday nights Alexa gets to stay up late.
   excited   sad   dizzy

5 Amy ran to the bus stop and got there just as the school bus came.
   sad   mad   glad

6 Tom has a lot of homework.
   unhappy   scared   joyful

7 The team wins the game.
   happy   disappointed   mad

8 The teacher spills the paint.
   annoyed   joyful   excited

9 The lady's brand-new car stops working.
   tired   surprised   thankful

10 The basketball players practiced so hard their muscles ached.
   tired   refreshed   content

Reading Skills • 1–2 © 2004 Creative Teaching Press

Picture Sequence

Sequencing

Look at the pictures. Connect the numbers to the birthday cakes to show the order or sequence of what happens to the cake.

  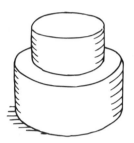 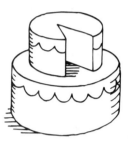

1   2   3   4

Look at the pictures. Connect the numbers to the pictures to show the order or sequence of a butterfly's lifecycle.

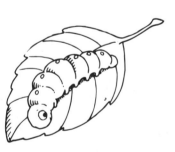  

1   2   3   4

Sequence Stories

Sequencing

A **sequence** is the order of things that happen in a story or situation.

Put the following sentences in order to tell a story.
Write a number 1 next to the sentence that is the first thing to happen in the sequence.
Write a number 2 next to the second thing to happen in the sequence.
Write a number 3 next to the third thing to happen in the sequence.

My Day

_____ In the evening, I did my homework.

_____ When I got up in the morning, I brushed my teeth.

_____ At lunchtime, I ate pizza.

Blowing a Bubble

Number the sentences from 1 to 4 to show the correct sequence.

_____ Next, I put it in my mouth.

_____ Finally, I blew a big bubble.

_____ First, I unwrapped the gum.

_____ Then, I chewed the gum until it was soft.

Reading Skills • 1–2 © 2004 Creative Teaching Press

Name _____

Sequence Fun

Sequencing

Fill in the blanks to describe the sequence of events that occur when you get ready for bed.

This is how I get ready for bed at _____. First, I
                                          (time)

_____. Then I have to _____.
        (action)   (action)

What comes next is that I _____ and finally
                                    (action)

_____.
     (action)

Fill in the blanks to describe the sequence of events that happen in your favorite fairy tale.

_____ upon a time, Cinderella _____.
(first word in a fairy tale)   (action or event)

What happened next is that _____.
                                    (action)

Then, _____.
              (action)

Later, _____.
              (action)

Finally, they lived happily ever _____.
                                      (ending word in a fairy tale)

My Life Chain of Events

Sequencing

Fill in the blank next to each area of the chain to describe events in the sequence of your life.

I was born on _____.

When I was a baby,

I _____.

By the age of _____, I could _____

_____.

In Kindergarten, my favorite thing to do was _____

_____.

I am in _____ grade now. On my next birthday,

I will be _____. When I am _____,

I would like to _____

_____.

Reading Skills • 1–2 © 2004 Creative Teaching Press

Sequencing Clues

Sequencing

There are words that act as clues to show the sequence of a set of events.

Read each sentence. Underline the words and phrases that help you sequence time.

1. Then, the baby started to cry.

2. In the afternoon, we went to the park.

3. First, I had to go to the store.

4. We feed the dog before we leave the house.

5. In the evening, I read a book.

6. The police finally arrived.

7. It had rained earlier.

8. Previously, we had been good friends.

9. They left for school in the morning.

10. Long ago, I lived in a two-story house.

11. After that it was time for clean up.

12. Once upon a time there was an old lady who lived in a shoe.

Conclusion Clues

Drawing Conclusions

An author does not always explain everything to a reader. A reader must sometimes use clues in order to figure out what is happening in a story or to answer questions. This is called **drawing conclusions.** Think of it like being a detective. You must use the clues to figure out what is happening. The clues can be in a sentence or in pictures.

Read each clue. Draw a conclusion and write your answer on the line.

1 A number between 7 and 10 that is not 8 _____

2 A letter between B and F that is the first letter in "cold" _____

3 A month that starts with "J" that is not in summer _____

4 A day of the week that starts with "T" and is not Thursday

_____

5 A word that rhymes with **cat** and **mat** and begins with "s"

_____

6 A four-sided figure that is the same shape as a door

_____

7 The color of an apple that is not yellow or green _____

8 What is in the sky at night that is not a star? _____

Conclusion Bubble

Drawing Conclusions

Read each sentence. Fill in the bubble next to the answer that is the best conclusion.

1 At the party everyone shouted, "Surprise!"
○ It was a Halloween party.
○ It was an Easter party.
○ It was a surprise birthday party.

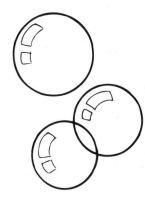

2 The car stopped because _____.
○ the light was red
○ the light was green
○ the light was purple

3 The girl had a fever.
○ She went to school.
○ She played basketball.
○ She rested and drank water.

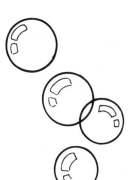

4 The boy's homework was not in his backpack.
○ The dog ate it.
○ He forgot to put it in his backpack.
○ A monkey stole it.

5 It was raining outside.
○ She wore a bathing suit.
○ She wore boots and brought an umbrella.
○ She wore high heels.

Name _____

Lola's Trouble

Drawing Conclusions

Read the story. Draw a conclusion and write your answer on the lines below.

One rainy afternoon, a girl named Lola went to the circus with her father, brother, and mother. Lola told her father what she wanted for a snack. Lola's father went to the snack bar and brought her cotton candy, popcorn, licorice, and a soda. Lola ate all of her snacks quickly. They were all gone by the time the circus was half over. During the second part of the circus, Lola did not feel well and wished she could go home.

The author does not tell us why Lola did not feel well, but the story provides clues. Draw a conclusion as to why Lola wanted to go home. Give a reason why you came to that conclusion.

Conclusion: _____

_____

_____

I came to this conclusion because _____

_____

_____

A Great Game

Drawing Conclusions

Carefully read the story. Draw a conclusion and answer the questions below.

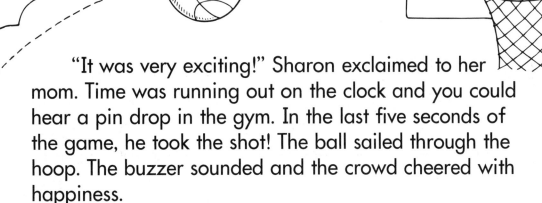

"It was very exciting!" Sharon exclaimed to her mom. Time was running out on the clock and you could hear a pin drop in the gym. In the last five seconds of the game, he took the shot! The ball sailed through the hoop. The buzzer sounded and the crowd cheered with happiness.

1 Where was Sharon? _____

2 What were the clue words that led you to that conclusion?

_____

3 Who do you think made the final basket? _____

4 Why did the crowd cheer with happiness? _____

_____

Picture Clues

Drawing Conclusions

Use the pictures as a clue to help you draw a conclusion. Circle your conclusion and tell why you made it.

It is raining.
It is a warm day.
It might snow.

I came to this conclusion because _____

_____.

It is the Fourth of July.
It is someone's birthday.
It is Thanksgiving.

I came to this conclusion because _____

_____.

The race was a tie.
The race was very close.
One turtle was faster than the other.

I came to this conclusion because _____

_____.

Reading Skills • 1–2 © 2004 Creative Teaching Press

Detail Decisions

Main Idea and Details

In each paragraph you read there is a main idea that tells what the paragraph is about. The details help readers understand more about the main idea.

Cross out the details that do not give information about the main idea.

Main Idea

Dogs make great pets.

Details
- Dogs can sit and roll over.
- The cat's name is Tom.
- Dogs can help protect you.

Main Idea

There are many kinds of flowers

Details
- Roses are red flowers.
- Violets are blue flowers.
- I like trees.

Explain why you chose the two details you crossed out.

_____

_____.

Main Idea and Details Web

Main Idea and Details

Making a web can help you organize the main idea and details when you are planning a story.

Think of a main idea and write it in the center circle. Think of four details about your main idea and write them in the smaller circles.

Example

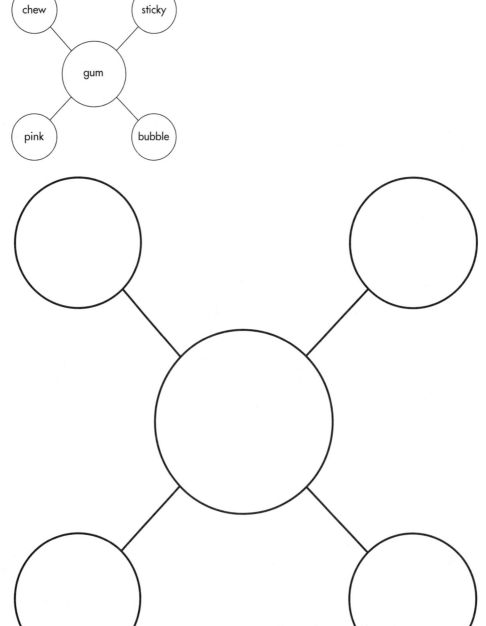

Name _____

Identifying the Main Idea and Details

Main Idea and Details

Read the paragraph. Underline the sentence that presents the main idea and write it on the lines below. Then write two details from the paragraph.

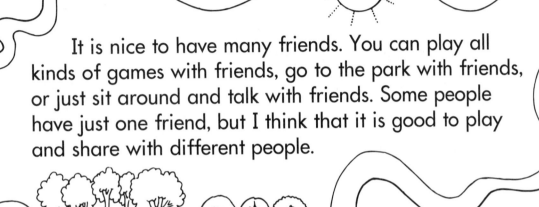

It is nice to have many friends. You can play all kinds of games with friends, go to the park with friends, or just sit around and talk with friends. Some people have just one friend, but I think that it is good to play and share with different people.

The main idea is _____

_____

One detail about friends is _____

Another detail about friends is _____

_____

_____

Name _____

The Main Message

Main Idea and Details

Cross out the pictures that do not show details about the main idea.

Main Idea: Summer

Main Idea: Transportation

Main Idea: Zoo

Deciding Details

Main Idea and Details

Write three detail sentences for each main idea.

Main Idea: Every morning I do three things.

Detail: _____

Detail: _____

Detail: _____

Main Idea: There are three reasons why I like school.

Detail: _____

Detail: _____

Detail: _____

Main Idea: I have many hobbies.

Detail: _____

Detail: _____

Detail: _____

Fill It In

Context Clues

Read each sentence. Choose the item that best completes the sentence. Write it on the line.

cupcake	ice cream	bee
key	sandwich	bus
cereal	pencil	plane

1 I put frosting on the _____.

2 I used the _____ to unlock the door.

3 The _____ flew to the hive.

4 I used a _____ to write my answers on the test.

5 I ate a _____ for lunch.

6 I ate _____ for breakfast.

7 I ate _____ for dessert.

8 I rode on the _____ to go to school.

9 I rode on the _____ to get from Texas to New York.

Reading Skills • 1–2 © 2004 Creative Teaching Press

Name _____

The Best Choice

Context Clues

Circle the word that best completes each sentence.

1 I took a _____ with my new camera.

    rest   envelope
    picture   ride

2 It was very cold, so I put on _____.

    shorts   a jacket
    a bathing suit the radio

3 I saw _____ swimming by our boat.

    dogs   goats
    giraffes   fish

4 I read two _____ this week.

    skates   books
    apples   cars

5 I _____ to my grandma on the telephone.

    talked   followed
    ran   ate

6 Some _____ can be trained to talk.

    trains   radios
    parrots   plants

Name _____

What's My Job?

Context Clues

Read the clues. Match each job with the correct clue.

_____ **1** I take your order and bring the food to the table.

_____ **2** I take care of animals.

_____ **3** I gather the news and tell people about it.

_____ **4** I deliver letters and packages.

_____ **5** I put out fires.

_____ **6** I cut people's hair.

_____ **7** I plan lessons and grade papers.

_____ **8** I write books.

_____ **9** I check people's teeth.

_____ **10** I prepare and cook food.

a. author

b. mail carrier

c. chef

d. barber

e. dentist

f. teacher

g. waitress

h. veterinarian

i. reporter

j. firefighter

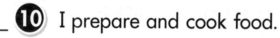

Reading Skills • 1–2 © 2004 Creative Teaching Press

Name _____

Name the Animal

Context Clues

Read each sentence. Choose the animal that best completes the sentence. Write it on the line.

| horse | pig | zebra | giraffe | eagle |
| lion | dog | duck | kangaroo | cat |

1 My _____ barks very loudly.

2 The _____ lives in a sty on the farm.

3 I rode a _____ on the trails in the hills.

4 The _____ purred and meowed.

5 The long neck of a _____ helps it to reach food.

6 The _____ soared through the sky.

7 I like the black and white stripes of the _____.

8 I saw a _____ swimming in the pond.

9 Look at the _____ with its baby in its pouch.

10 The _____ let out a ferocious roar.

Make a Sandwich

Categorizing Events and Ideas

Read the words in the box. Choose the words that help you describe how to make a peanut butter and jelly sandwich. Write the words on the lines.

cheese	fork	bread	apple	knife
bagel	spread	jelly	stir	peanut butter

1 _____

2 _____

3 _____

4 _____

5 _____

Use the five words to write a description of how to make a peanut butter and jelly sandwich.

_____

_____

_____

_____

Reading Skills • 1–2 © 2004 Creative Teaching Press

School Categories

Categorizing Events and Ideas

Read the words in the box. Decide which part of a school you would most likely find each item. Write the items in the matching columns.

student	computer	secretary	stapler	principal
slide	ball	math book	teacher	jump rope
letters	ruler	copy machine	chalk	

Classroom	Playground	Office

Choose a Category

Categorizing Events and Ideas

When you sort people and things into groups, it helps you organize information for better understanding. This is called **categorizing**.

Read the words on each crayon. Circle the category that they belong in.

colors
fruits
candy

red   black   pink

winged animals
furry animals
scaly animals

rabbits   cats   dogs

vegetables
plants
fruits

apple   plum   orange

fairy tales
numbers
animals

8   6   7

numbers
colors
shapes

circle   square   triangle

Pick a Category

Categorizing Events and Ideas

Read the words in each box. Circle the category that best describes the words.

1
| Sour |
| Sweet |
| Salty |
| Bitter |

Things I see
Things I taste
Things I wear
Books I read

5
| Basketball |
| Soccer |
| Tennis |
| Golf |

Food
Sports
Time
Crafts

2
| Laughing |
| Barking |
| Ringing |
| Buzzing |

Time
Weather
Things I feel
Things I hear

6
| Cloudy |
| Windy |
| Fog |
| Rain |

Weather
Time
Things I hear
Seasons

3
| Trees |
| Clouds |
| Cups |
| Tables |

Fruits
Weather
Things I see
Things I taste

7
| Book |
| Report |
| Poem |
| Story |

Things I read
Rhymes
Things I feel
Sports

4
| Cinnamon |
| Chocolate |
| Bread |
| Ice cream |

Things I taste
Things I feel
Things in the yard
Things in a car

8
| Furry |
| Rough |
| Soft |
| Prickly |

Things I feel
Toys
Things I hear
Seasons

Sound Categorization

Categorizing Events and Ideas

Categorize the words by beginning blends. Write each word in the matching box.

stride	from	freedom	clog	clean
frog	clap	front	stop	stuck
free	stood	fright	clip	closet
clover	stamp	stick	Friday	strong

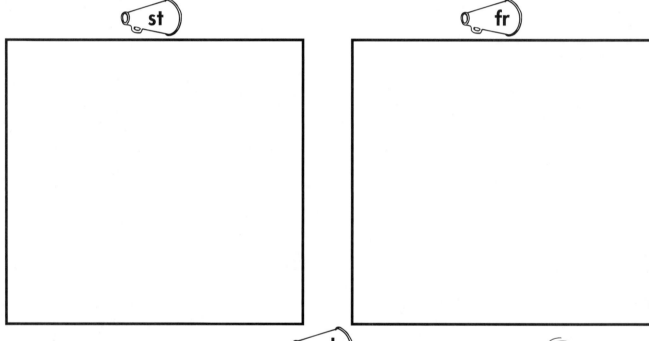

st

fr

cl

Reading Skills • 1–2 © 2004 Creative Teaching Press

Story Element Bubble

Story Elements

An author describes places, people, and events in a story so that the reader will understand the story better. The setting, characters, and problems, or conflicts, in a story are called the **story elements**.
- The **setting** is the time and place of the story.
- The **conflict** is usually one or more problems that the characters are having in the story.
- The characters look for ways to solve their problems.
- The **characters** are people or animals in the story.

Fill in the bubble next to the setting, character, or problem. You may need to fill in more than one in each box.

Setting	Character	Problem
○ forest	○ monkey	○ lost in a storm
○ door	○ girl	○ trash can
○ apple	○ shirt	○ a nice new house
○ zoo	○ old man	○ mean neighbors

Setting	Character	Problem
○ mice	○ stair	○ a hard test
○ once upon a time	○ princess	○ a sunny day
○ in a castle	○ horse	○ a clock
○ a baby	○ hair	○ shoe

Jack and Jill Story Elements

Story Elements

- The **setting** is the time and place of the story.
- The **conflict** is usually one or more problems that the characters are having in the story.
- The characters look for ways to solve their problems.
- The **characters** are people or animals in the story.

Read the poem. Then fill in the story map by listing the characters, setting, problem, and ending.

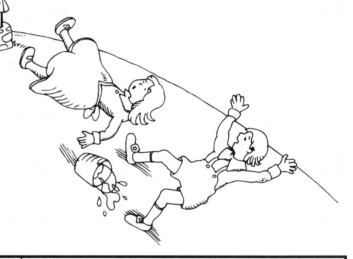

Jack and Jill went up the hill
To fetch a pail of water.
Jack fell down and broke
His crown
And Jill came
Tumbling after!

Characters	Setting
Problem	**Ending**

Story Element Identification

Story Elements

Read the descriptions for each story. Write **Setting**, **Problem**, or **Character** on the line to identify each story element.

Goldilocks and the Three Bears

1 _____ Goldilocks

2 _____ little house in the woods

3 _____ The bears' house was a mess.

4 _____ three bears

5 _____ the bedroom upstairs in the three bears' house

6 _____ The baby bear's oatmeal was gone.

Jack and the Beanstalk

7 _____ giant

8 _____ giant's wife

9 _____ goose that laid the golden egg

10 _____ giant's castle

11 _____ Jack and his mom have no money.

Name the Element

Story Elements

Look at each picture. Write **Setting, Problem,** or **Character** to identify the story element the picture represents.

_____

_____

_____

_____

_____

_____

Story Element Web

Story Elements

Pretend you are going to write a story. You want to make sure you include all of the story elements. Fill in the web with details about your story.

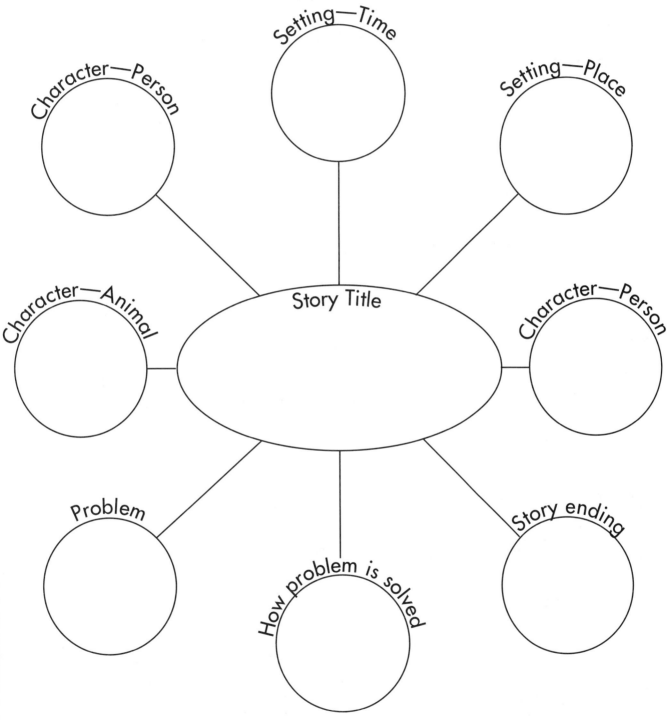

Use your completed web to help you write your story on the back of this paper.

Name _____

Reality and Fantasy Fill-In

Reality and Fantasy

When an author is telling about something that is make-believe, it is called **fantasy**. When an author is telling about something that can actually happen, it is called **reality**.

Read the sentences. Write **Reality** if the sentence describes something that could actually happen. Write **Fantasy** if the sentence describes something make-believe.

1 Children played games on the computer. _____

2 The child set the table for dinner. _____

3 The dad gave the baby a bottle. _____

4 A fish could talk. _____

5 The ant and elephant held hands. _____

6 The pot lifted off the counter and flew into the air.

_____

7 The kids walked to school. _____

8 A lion drove a car. _____

9 It rained hot dogs. _____

10 The park was filled with children. _____

11 The telephone rang. _____

Reading Skills • 1–2 © 2004 Creative Teaching Press

Name _____

Write a Reality

Reality and Fantasy

Fill in the blank in each sentence with a word that would make the sentence a reality.
Remember that reality is something that could actually happen.

1 She hit the ball and _____.

2 _____ in the big house.

3 The alligator lived in a _____.

4 He swam to the _____.

5 The team _____ when they won the game.

6 The teacher was excited when the class _____.

7 "I want _____," cried the baby.

8 At the market you can buy _____.

9 At the movies you can eat _____.

10 The color of the flower was _____.

11 Dogs can _____.

12 In the park there is _____.

Fantastic Fantasies

Reality and Fantasy

Complete each sentence with a word that would make the sentence make-believe or a fantasy.

1 The backpack was filled with _____.

2 The _____ all lived in a suitcase.

3 The musician used a _____ to play music.

4 Her mom said, " You may have _____ cookies."

5 The _____ could talk.

6 The sky was the color _____.

7 _____ was found growing in the garden.

8 _____ lived in the barn.

9 The pool was filled with _____.

10 A _____ can fly.

11 The kangaroo hopped to the _____.

12 The computer _____.

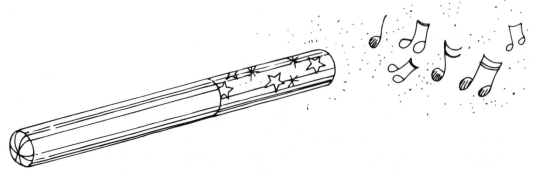

Reading Skills • 1–2 © 2004 Creative Teaching Press

Name _____

Reality and Fantasy Fun

Reality and Fantasy

For each word write one reality and one fantasy sentence.
Example: The <u>boat</u> sailed on the water.
The <u>boat</u> flew high in the sky.

flower

Reality_____

Fantasy_____

bubble gum

Reality_____

Fantasy_____

beetle

Reality_____

Fantasy_____

banana

Reality_____

Fantasy_____

night time

Reality_____

Fantasy_____

Name _____

Castle Coloring

Reality and Fantasy

Stories we read are often part fantasy and part reality or have parts that are make-believe and parts that could be real.

Read the description in each part of the castle. If the description is a fantasy, color that part yellow. If the description is a reality, color that part orange.

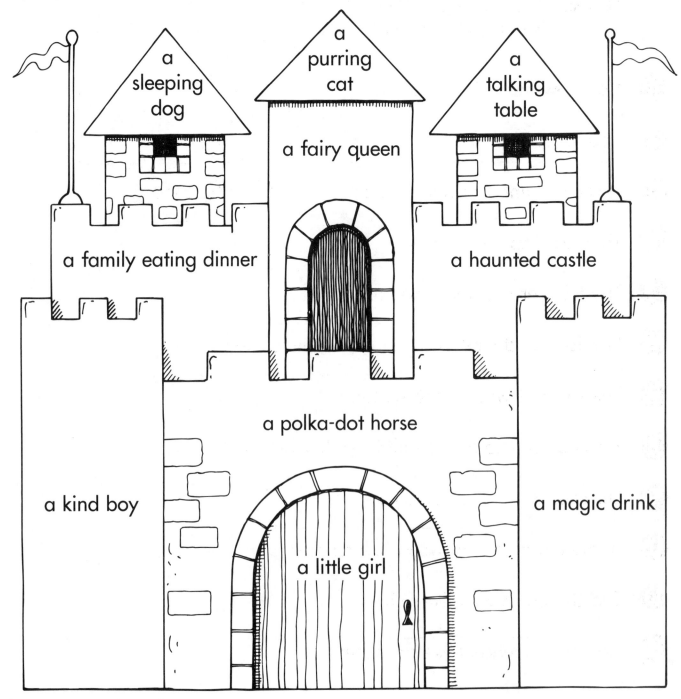

a sleeping dog

a purring cat

a talking table

a fairy queen

a family eating dinner

a haunted castle

a polka-dot horse

a kind boy

a magic drink

a little girl

Simile Clues

Similes

> Authors sometimes use **similes** to compare two things using the clue words *like* or *as*. Figurative language can help the reader understand the point the author is trying to make.

Underline the clue word or words used to make the comparison in each sentence.

Example: He can run <u>like</u> the wind.
Ken was <u>as</u> busy <u>as</u> a bee.

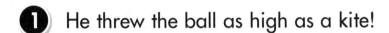

1 He threw the ball as high as a kite!

2 You fought like a champ!

3 Lisa can climb like a monkey!

4 The dog slept like a rock.

5 The teacher was as happy as a lark.

6 Her forehead was as warm as a summer day.

7 The sweater was as soft as fur.

8 Andrea felt like a frisky kitten at her birthday party.

9 His cheeks were as red as a rose.

10 In the morning, Tim walks like his feet are made of lead.

11 The children swam like fish.

12 Her voice sounded like an angel.

Find the Similes

Similes

Read the paragraph from "'Twas the Night Before Christmas." Underline three comparisons using the words *like* or *as*. Draw a picture of one of the phrases that you underlined.

His eyes, how they twinkled! His dimples, how merry!
His cheeks were like roses, his nose like a cherry!
His droll little mouth was drawn up in a bow,
And the beard on his chin was as white as the snow.

Reading Skills • 1–2 © 2004 Creative Teaching Press

What's Being Compared?

Similes

Draw a box around the two things being compared in each sentence.

1 The cow was as thin as a rail.

2 The monster was as fat as a pig.

3 Emily was as sly as a fox.

4 The soap flew out of my hands like a slippery fish.

5 That toddler was as stubborn as a mule.

6 Like a hungry lion, Matthew attacked his lunch.

7 His legs were like rubber bands after playing football on Saturday.

8 My room was as bright as the sun.

9 The audience looked like statues, sitting so still in their seats.

10 Today the clouds are as white as the snow.

What Does It Really Mean?

Similes

Read each sentence. Explain in your own words what point the author is trying to make.

1 Emily is as sharp as a tack.

_____

_____

2 Abby is as hungry as a horse.

_____

_____

3 The thief was as quiet as a mouse.

_____

_____

4 Claire's cheeks were as red as a rose.

_____

_____

5 Ben climbed like a monkey.

_____

_____

Reading Skills • 1–2 © 2004 Creative Teaching Press

Simile Crossword Puzzle

Similes

Authors sometimes use **similes** to compare two things using the clue words *like* or *as*. Similes can help the reader understand the point the author is trying to make.

Use the words in the box to complete the clues and fill in the crossword puzzle.

fish	horse	monkey	snake
happy	warm	whip	

Across

1. She slithered like a _____.
2. She was as hungry as a _____.
3. Her mind was as sharp as a _____.

Down

2. The baby was as _____ as a lark.
3. His forehead was as _____ as a summer day.
4. He could swim like a _____.
5. The child could climb like a _____.

Reading Skills • 1-2 © 2004 Creative Teaching Press

Name _____

Bear Party

Following Directions

Follow the directions to color the bear.

- Color the bear's shirt green.
- Color the bear's face, arms, and legs brown.
- Color the bear's hat blue.
- Color the present red.
- Color the horn orange.
- Draw red, blue, green, and yellow streamers and confetti around the bear.

Secret Message

Following Directions

Follow the directions to reveal the secret message.

1 Cross out the letter **a.**

2 Cross out the letter **d.**

3 Cross out the letter **z.**

4 Change the **m** to a **k.**

5 Change the **y**'s to **o**'s

aIdz alzdiame scahdyayazl.

Now write the letters on the lines below to reveal the secret message.

___ ___ ___ ___ ___ ___ ___ ___ .

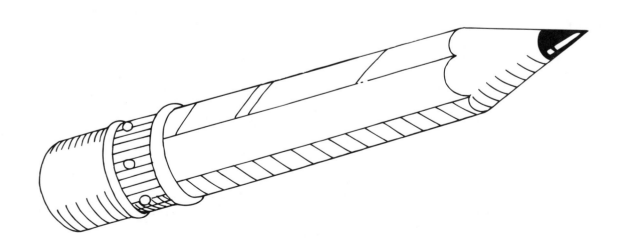

Reading Skills • 1–2 © 2004 Creative Teaching Press

Name _____

Riddle Fun

Following Directions

Follow the directions to reveal the answer to the riddle.

Why is a giraffe the cheapest pet to feed?

1 Write the word **way** on line 10

2 Write the word **feed** on line 3.

3 Write the word **little** on line 6.

4 Write the word **a** on lines 5 and 8.

5 Write the word **goes** on line 7.

6 Write the word **it** on line 4.

7 Write the word **you** on line 2.

8 Write the word **When** on line 1.

9 Write the word **long** on line 9.

Answer:

_____   _____   _____   _____   _____
   1   2   3   4   5

_____   _____   _____   _____   _____!
   6   7   8   9   10

Reading Skills • 1–2 © 2004 Creative Teaching Press

Fishing for a Sentence

Following Directions

Follow the directions to reveal the secret sentence.

1 Cross out all the number words.

2 Cross out all the words that begin with the letter **l**.

3 Cross out all the color words.

Now unscramble the remaining words and write the sentence below.

_____ .

Name _____

Synonym Analogies

Analogies

An **analogy** is a relationship between two pairs of words. Some analogies use synonyms (words that mean the same thing).

> **Example:** <u>tiny</u> is to <u>small</u> as <u>big</u> is to <u>huge</u>
>
> The first two words, *tiny* and *small*, mean the same thing.
> The second pair of words, *big* and *huge*, mean the same thing.
> Both pairs of words are related in the same way; both pairs of words are synonyms.

Fill in the bubble next to the word that best completes each analogy.

1 <u>floppy</u> is to <u>limp</u> as <u>ill</u> is to _____
- ○ well
- ○ sick
- ○ healthy
- ○ fine

2 <u>odor</u> is to <u>smell</u> as <u>small</u> is to _____
- ○ big
- ○ little
- ○ massive
- ○ tall

3 <u>mend</u> is to <u>fix</u> as <u>easy</u> is to _____
- ○ early
- ○ hard
- ○ difficult
- ○ simple

4 <u>piece</u> is to <u>part</u> as <u>fast</u> is to _____
- ○ quick
- ○ slow
- ○ happy
- ○ small

5 <u>toss</u> is to <u>throw</u> as <u>pain</u> is to _____
- ○ push
- ○ ache
- ○ shot
- ○ plain

6 <u>late</u> is to <u>tardy</u> as <u>close</u> is to _____
- ○ away
- ○ distant
- ○ far
- ○ near

Reading Skills • 1–2 © 2004 Creative Teaching Press

Antonym Analogies

Analogies

An **analogy** is a relationship between two pairs of words. Some analogies use antonyms (words that have the opposite meaning).

> **Example:** <u>large</u> is to <u>small</u> as <u>loud</u> is to <u>quiet</u>

> The first two words, *large* and *small,* are opposites.
> The second pair of words, *loud* and *quiet,* are opposites.
> Both pairs of words are related in the same way; both pairs of words are antonyms.

Fill in the bubble next to the word that best completes each analogy.

1 <u>cold</u> is to <u>hot</u> as <u>ill</u> is to _____
- ○ fever
- ○ sick
- ○ healthy
- ○ happy

2 <u>slow</u> is to <u>fast</u> as <u>small</u> is to _____
- ○ big
- ○ little
- ○ tiny
- ○ medium

3 <u>break</u> is to <u>repair</u> as <u>easy</u> is to _____
- ○ early
- ○ fun
- ○ difficult
- ○ simple

4 <u>whole</u> is to <u>part</u> as <u>start</u> is to _____
- ○ quick
- ○ stop
- ○ happy
- ○ go

5 <u>dry</u> is to <u>wet</u> as <u>hero</u> is to _____
- ○ push
- ○ friend
- ○ good
- ○ villain

6 <u>late</u> is to <u>early</u> as <u>close</u> is to _____
- ○ open
- ○ shut
- ○ slam
- ○ near

Rhyming Analogies
Analogies

Use a word from the box to complete each rhyming analogy.

log	cheek	pink	trunk	fly
best	rock	thank	rent	none

1 <u>cat</u> is to <u>rat</u> as <u>dog</u> is to _____

2 <u>pig</u> is to <u>wig</u> as <u>clock</u> is to _____

3 <u>pen</u> is to <u>ten</u> as <u>tent</u> is to _____

4 <u>bear</u> is to <u>chair</u> as <u>sink</u> is to _____

5 <u>room</u> is to <u>broom</u> as <u>nest</u> is to _____

6 <u>pin</u> is to <u>win</u> as <u>dunk</u> is to _____

7 <u>trick</u> is to <u>kick</u> as <u>eye</u> is to _____

8 <u>ball</u> is to <u>fall</u> as <u>weak</u> is to _____

9 <u>fit</u> is to <u>mitt</u> as <u>sun</u> is to _____

10 <u>bug</u> is to <u>hug</u> as <u>tank</u> is to _____

Name _____

Analogy Mix-Up

Analogies

Use a word from the box to complete each analogy.

sour	look	rush	off	cold
fly	noisy	shake	pretty	hard

1 small is to tiny as hurry is to _____

2 nice is to mean as hot is to _____

3 came is to blame as book is to _____

4 fast is to slow as on is to _____

5 ill is to sick as beautiful is to _____

6 late is to tardy as loud is to _____

7 trick is to kick as eye is to _____

8 sad is to happy as sweet is to _____

9 loud is to quiet as soft is to _____

10 bring is to thing as cake is to _____

Answer Key

Starting Sounds (page 5)

slide	store	clown
snail	sky	bread
stick	skunk	cloud

Consonant Blend Tally (page 6)

Consonant Blend	Tally	Total
cr	II	2
gr	III	3
bl	IIII	4
fl	III	3
pr	I	1
tr	IIII	5
pl	III	3
gl	I	1

tr had the most tally marks

The Blend That Does Not Belong (page 7)

1. drip
2. clutter
3. frill
4. smell
5. sweater

Find the Blend (page 8)

1. twinkle
2. star
3. where
4. sky

1. frogs
2. speckled
3. where
4. green
5. glub

Fill in the Blend (page 9)

1. bring
2. broom
3. crib
4. princess
5. blanket
6. dress
7. drum
8. frost
9. crab
10. fruit

X Marks the Sound (page 10)

Long Vowels

/a/	X	X	X	X	X	X	X				
/e/	X	X	X	X	X						
/i/	X	X	X	X							
/o/	X	X	X	X	X	X					
/u/	X	X									

Which long vowel sound did you hear the most? _____a_____

Word Change (page 11)

tap	tip	top
hat	hit	hot
rack	rick	rock
pat	pit	pot
black	blick	block

Blick is a nonsense word.

Sentences will vary.

Sound Bubble (page 12)

bowl—o	mule—u	lake—a
nine—i	dish— i	hot—o
green—e	bat— a	bug—u
	pen—e	

Missing Middle (page 13)

ea	oa	ea	oa
ea	oo	ou	oo
oo	ou	oo	ea

Short Seesaw Sounds (page 14)

a—bat, lap
e—hen, met
i—pin, fish
o—not, pop
u—cup, fun

Watermelon Words (page 15)

Answers will vary. Possible answers include:

car—star
cub—cab
sad—head
ox—six
man—hen
flop—hop
fell—ball
sick—truck

It's a Match (page 16)

m—game, dime
e—kitty, daddy
l—hole, stole
i—sky, butterfly

Finish the Word (page 17)

x	l	g
p	n	k
r	t	d

Circle the Sound (page 18)

v	x	p
n	sh	r
ch	n	k

Ending Sound Bubble (page 19)

candy—e	dumb—m	phone—n
my—i	ride—d	they—a
	play—a	

Rhyme in a Line (page 20)

1. sun
2. hand
3. line
4. net
5. dock
6. catch
7. found
8. must
9. hike
10. heat
11. bake
12. flight

Rhyming Clues (page 21)

1. look
2. hair
3. tooth
4. door
5. light
6. jug
7. feet
8. had
9. cake
10. sit
11. bird
12. broom

Bubble Time Rhyme (page 22)

smell	bat	tree	cheek
desk	bee	apple	snail
had	tan		

Nursery Time Rhymes (page 23)

Jill—hill
down—crown
diddle—fiddle
moon—spoon
Horner—corner
pie—I
thumb—plumb

Rhyme Time (page 24)

1. hand
2. band
3. stand
4. land
5. sand
6. strand

Sight Word Search (page 25)

<u>Lost</u>
four
eight
once

<u>Found</u>
some
very
seven
pull
out

<u>Wanted</u>
who
could
walk
two

<u>Car for Sale</u>
want
only
come
once

Fill in the Sight Word (page 26)

1. your
2. Do
3. half
4. eight
5. wrote
6. have
7. again
8. said
9. you
10. from
11. Climb
12. eyes

See the Sight Words (page 27)

only	once	were	was	to	you
II	II	III	III	ℍℍ II	II

word found most often: to

Sight Word Study (page 28)

3-Letter Sight Words
are, for, one, was, you

4-Letter Sight Words
come, eyes, from, have, pull, said, they

Words That Begin with a Vowel
are, again, eyes, one, other, of

Words That End with a Vowel
are, come, do, have, one, you

Common Sight Words (page 29)

climb	eight	eyes
four	half	seven
two	water	one

Combine the Compound (page 30)

baseball

cupcake

classroom

homework

starfish

sailboat

airplane

outside

backpack

birdbath

bluebird

playpen

Can You Find the Compounds? (page 31)

1. grandmother
2. grandson
3. homework
4. newspaper
5. paintbrush
6. notebook
7. blueberry
8. cupcake
9. popcorn
10. backpack
11. classroom

Compound Clues (page 32)

1. homework
2. paintbrush
3. popcorn
4. sailboat
5. newspaper
6. basketball
7. snowman
8. backpack
9. raincoat
10. doghouse
11. snowstorm
12. mailbox

Compound Crossword (page 33)

Across

1. anthill
2. horsefly
4. starfish
6. teapot
7. playpen

Down

1. airplane
3. lighthouse
5. baseball

Fill in the Compound (page 34)

1. afternoon
2. sunshine
3. birthday
4. outside
5. football
6. swimsuit
7. barnyard
8. anyone
9. firefighter
10. rainbow
11. campground
12. inside

Word Family Bubble (page 35)

hen	see	yes
zoo	yellow	goes
mine	back	swim

Finish the Family (page 36)

game	nut	skate
rose	boat	sock
gum	bell	dice

Form a Family (page 37)

rain, grain, brain, gain

mail, sail, fail, rail

mole, sole, hole, whole

truck, buck, duck, stuck

van, pan, ran, fan

hill, will, fill, bill

lit, bit, spit, hit

rig, pig, big

jet, met, pet, let

Family Riddles (-ug) (page 38)

1. bug
2. tug
3. lug
4. hug
5. dug
6. jug

Possible answers include: met and pet

Family Riddles (-ain) (page 39)

1. chain
2. main
3. gain
4. pain
5. rain
6. Spain

Possible answers include: math and path

Make It Make Sense (page 40)

1. shake
2. duck
3. sink
4. fall
5. duck
6. pen
7. note
8. fall
9. sink
10. pen
11. note
12. shake

Which Meaning Makes Sense? (page 41)

1. to put dishes on the table
2. a container that holds something
3. to sway back and forth
4. upper part of the legs when sitting
5. to fall
6. to bump into something with force

Answers will vary.

Multiple Meaning Crossword Puzzle (page 42)

Across

1. pick
2. bed
3. pants

Down

2. band
3. pit
4. shine
5. back

Multiple Meaning Sentences (page 43)

Answers will vary. Possible answers include:

seal

1. The seal balanced a ball on its nose.
2. I used a sticker to seal the envelope.

spring

1. Some beds have spiral springs inside.
2. Many flowers bloom during spring.

shake

1. I drank a chocolate shake.
2. I shake the present to try to guess what's inside.

Multiple Meaning Clues (page 44)

1. ring
2. match
3. sock
4. tick
5. cap

Similar Synonyms (page 45)

small
little
tiny

scream
yell
shout

big
giant
large

nice
kind
pleasant

make
create
build

box
carton
container

cool
cold
chilly

cry
sob
weep

Synonym Balls (page 46)

Color: said/told; cap/hat; jog/run; pal/friend;
gift/present; finish/end

Antonym Seesaws (page 47)

Color: up/down; alive/dead; yes/no; in/out; top/bottom

Fill in the Antonym (page 48)

1. shut
2. hot
3. awake
4. tall
5. off
6. old
7. sad
8. brother
9. no
10. thick

Similar and Opposite (page 49)

good	great	bad
town	city	country
cool	cold	hot
happy	glad	sad
kind	nice	mean
messy	dirty	clean
little	small	big
fast	quick	slow
smile	grin	frown

You Choose (page 50)

1. ate
2. flower
3. hair
4. aunt
5. sent
6. Do
7. blew
8. see
9. deer
10. two
11. bee
12. won

Label It (page 51)

1. tail
2. tea
3. rose
4. clothes
5. four
6. sun

Fill in the Homophone (page 52)

1. buy
2. know
3. hour
4. see
5. There
6. by
7. sea
8. our
9. their
10. no

Homophone Search (page 53)

sun	to	son
see	too	their
eight	there	sea
two	ate	so
week	do	rode
would	hours	

Prefix Fill-In (page 54)

1. disobey
2. misspell
3. unsafe
4. Untie
5. repay
6. preschool
7. refill

Prefix Production (page 55)

1. refold—fold again
2. retell—tell again
3. presoak—soak before
4. reread—read again
5. uneaten—not eaten
6. misunderstood—not understood

Answers will vary. Possible answers include:
7. recall
8. reuse
9. mishandle
10. untold
11. unlucky
12. preview

13. retake
14. unfinished
15. remove
16. pretest

Suffix Fill-In (page 56)

1. painful
2. nicely
3. useless
4. fuller
5. helpless
6. happier
7. powerful

Suffix Sentences (page 57)

1. loudly—in a loud way
2. helpful—full of help
3. redder—more red
4. foolishly—in a foolish way
5. fearless—without fear
6. cheerful—full of cheer

Answers will vary. Possible answers include:
7. hopeful or hopeless
8. stronger
9. thoughtless or thoughtful
10. childish
11. agreement

Base Words (page 58)

1. prefix   fair
2. suffix   like
3. suffix   big
4. suffix   happy
5. prefix   name
6. suffix   thick
7. suffix   child
8. suffix   cheer
9. prefix   use
10. prefix   cut
11. prefix   start
12. suffix   quick

Match the Contraction Pairs (page 59)

we are	we're
he is	he's
you are	you're
we have	we've
she is	she's
they will	they'll
will not	won't
they are	they're
do not	don't
you have	you've
is not	isn't
they have	they've

Character Contractions (page 60)

1. can't	can not
2. aren't	are not
3. he'll	he will
4. I'll	I will
5. I'm	I am
6. She's	she is
7. Who's	who is
8. You've	you have
9. Let's	let us
10. You'll, you're	you will, you are

Contraction Choice (page 61)

1. don't
2. wasn't
3. couldn't
4. We're
5. They're
6. He's
7. hadn't
8. wouldn't
9. can't
10. She'll
11. I've
12. won't

Contraction Cross-Out (page 62)

call	I	cold
will	shirt	well
week	do	ill
like	cold	they

Contraction Search (page 63)

Underline: can't, I'm, shouldn't, you'll, I'll, she'll, we've, you're, It's, doesn't, won't

1. won't, we've
2. can not
3. I'll, I'm
4. can't, shouldn't, doesn't, won't

Prediction Practice (page 64)

1. The vase is going to fall.
2. He is going to fall asleep.
3. The child cries.
4. It will rain.
5. He will dive into the pool.
6. The baby birds will eat.
7. She will ask her parents if she can have a puppy.

Sensible Predictions (page 65)

These clouds should be colored:
The dog will be taken for a walk.
The baby's mother will give him soft food.
The birthday girl will blow out the candles.
They will go camping for the weekend.

School Predictions (page 66)

Answers will vary. Possible answers include:
1. Probably more students will get chicken pox.
2. The students will return when they're feeling better.
3. The field trip will be postponed.
4. They will probably win tonight.

Prediction Puzzlers (page 67)

1. Suzie
2. Yellow
3. Answers will vary.
4. Answers will vary.

Predicting Feelings (page 68)

1. scared
2. sad
3. startled
4. excited
5. glad
6. unhappy
7. happy
8. annoyed
9. surprised
10. tired

Picture Sequence (page 69)

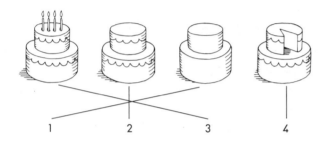

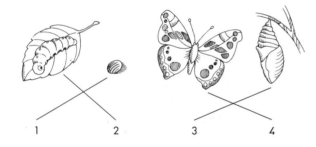

Sequence Stories (page 70)

My Day
3
1
2

Blowing a Bubble
2
4
1
3

Sequence Fun (page 71)

Answers will vary. Possible answers include:
This is how I get ready for bed at <u>night.</u> First,
<u>I put on my pajamas.</u> Then I have to <u>wash my face.</u>
What comes next is that I <u>brush my teeth</u>, and finally
I <u>climb into bed</u>.

<u>Once</u> upon a time, Cinderella <u>met a prince</u>. What
happened next was that <u>she lost her slipper</u>. Then,
<u>the prince looked for her</u>. Later, <u>he found her and
married her</u>. Finally, they lived happily ever <u>after</u>.

My Life Chain of Events (page 72)

Answers will vary.

Sequencing Clues (page 73)

1. Then
2. In the afternoon
3. First
4. before we leave
5. In the evening
6. finally
7. earlier
8. Previously
9. in the morning
10. Long ago
11. After
12. Once upon a time

Conclusion Clues (page 74)

1. 9
2. c
3. January
4. Tuesday
5. sat
6. rectangle
7. red
8. moon

Conclusion Bubble (page 75)

1. It was a surprise birthday party.
2. the light was red
3. She rested and drank water.
4. He forgot to put it in his backpack.
5. She wore boots and brought an umbrella.

Lola's Trouble (page 76)

Answers will vary. Possible answer:

Conclusion: The snacks Lola ate made her stomach upset. I came to this conclusion because all her snacks were junk foods and she ate them really fast.

A Great Game (page 77)

1. a basketball game
2. Answers will vary. Possible answers include: gym, game, shot, hoop
3. the basketball player
4. Answers will vary. Possible answer:
   The home team must have won.

Picture Clues (page 78)

1. It is a warm day.
   Answers will vary.
2. It is someone's birthday.
   Answers will vary.
3. One turtle was much faster than the other.
   Answers will vary.

Detail Decisions (page 79)

The cat's name is Tom.
I like trees.
The cat's name has nothing to do with how dogs make great pets.
The main idea is about flowers, not trees.

Main Idea and Details Web (page 80)

Webs will vary.

Identifying the Main Idea and Details (page 81)

It is nice to have many friends.
Answers will vary. Possible answers include: you can play, go to the park, sit around, talk

The Main Message (page 82)

Cross out jacket, cookies and milk
Cross out telephone, book
Cross out apple, basketball

Deciding Details (page 83)

Answers will vary.

Fill It In (page 84)

1. cupcake
2. key
3. bee
4. pencil
5. sandwich
6. cereal
7. ice cream
8. bus
9. plane

The Best Choice (page 85)

1. picture
2. a jacket
3. fish
4. books
5. talked
6. parrots

What's My Job? (page 86)

1. g
2. h
3. i
4. b
5. j
6. d
7. f
8. a
9. e
10. c

Name the Animal (page 87)

1. dog
2. pig
3. horse
4. cat

5. giraffe
6. eagle
7. zebra
8. duck
9. kangaroo
10. lion

Make a Sandwich (page 88)

bread
knife
spread
jelly
peanut butter

Answers will vary. Possible answer:
Use a knife to spread peanut butter on one side of a piece of bread. Wipe the knife clean and use it to spread jelly on another piece of bread. Put the sticky sides together and enjoy!

School Categories (page 89)

Answers may vary. Possible answers include:

Classroom	Playground	Office
student	slide	letters
ruler	ball	computer
math book	jump rope	secretary
teacher		copy machine
chalk		principal
		stapler

Choose a Category (page 90)

colors
furry animals
fruits
numbers
shapes

Pick a Category (page 91)

1. Things I taste
2. Things I hear
3. Things I see
4. Things I taste
5. Sports
6. Weather
7. Things I read
8. Things I feel

Sound Categorization (page 92)

st
stride
stood
stick
stop
stuck
stamp
strong

fr
from
freedom
frog
front
free
fright
Friday

cl
clog
clean
clap
clip
closet
clover

Story Element Bubble (page 93)

Setting—forest, zoo
Character—monkey, girl, old man
Problem—lost in a storm, mean neighbors
Setting—once upon a time, in a castle
Character—princess, horse
Problem—a hard test

Jack and Jill Story Elements (page 94)

Characters—Jack and Jill
Setting—hill
Problem—Jack fell down and broke his crown
Ending—Jill came tumbling down, too.

Story Element Identification (page 95)

Goldilocks and the Three Bears

1. Character
2. Setting
3. Problem
4. Character
5. Setting
6. Problem

Jack and the Beanstalk

7. Character
8. Character
9. Character
10. Setting
11. Problem

Name the Element (page 96)

Setting
Problem or Character
Character
Setting
Character
Problem

Story Element Web (page 97)

Webs will vary.

Reality and Fantasy Fill-In (page 98)

1. Reality
2. Reality
3. Reality
4. Fantasy
5. Fantasy
6. Fantasy
7. Reality
8. Fantasy
9. Fantasy
10. Reality
11. Reality

Write a Reality (page 99)

Answers will vary.

Fantastic Fantasies (page 100)

Answers will vary.

Reality and Fantasy Fun (page 101)

Answers will vary.

Castle Coloring (page 102)

These parts of the castle should be colored yellow:
a polka-dot horse
a fairy queen
a talking table
a haunted castle
a magic drink

These parts of the castle should be colored orange:
a little girl
a sleeping dog
a kind boy
a purring cat
a family eating dinner

Simile Clues (page 103)

1. as high as a kite
2. fought like a champ
3. climb like a monkey
4. slept like a rock
5. as happy as a lark
6. as warm as a summer day
7. as soft as fur
8. felt like a frisky kitten
9. as red as a rose
10. walks like his feet are made of lead
11. swam like fish
12. sounded like an angel

Find the Similes (page 104)

His cheeks were like roses
his nose like a cherry
The beard on his chin was as white as the snow

What's Being Compared? (page 105)

1. cow, rail
2. monster, pig
3. Emily, fox
4. soap, fish
5. toddler, mule
6. Matthew, lion
7. legs, rubber bands
8. room, sun
9. audience, statues
10. clouds, snow

What Does It Really Mean? (page 106)

Answers will vary. Possible answers include:
1. Emily is a smart girl.
2. Abby is very hungry.
3. The thief made no noise.
4. Claire's cheeks were really red.
5. Ben is a good climber.

Simile Crossword Puzzle (page 107)

Across
1. snake
2. horse
3. whip

Down
2. happy
3. warm
4. fish
5. monkey

Bear Party (page 108)

Answers cannot be shown. Verify students have followed all directions.

Secret Message (page 109)

I like school.

Riddle Fun (page 110)

When you feed it a little goes a long way!

Fishing for a Sentence (page 111)

I go fishing every Sunday.

Synonym Analogies (page 112)

1. sick
2. little
3. simple
4. quick
5. ache
6. near

Antonym Analogies (page 113)

1. healthy
2. big
3. difficult
4. stop
5. villain
6. open

Rhyming Analogies (page 114)

1. log
2. rock
3. rent
4. pink
5. best
6. trunk
7. fly
8. cheek
9. none
10. thank

Analogy Mix-Up (page 115)

1. rush
2. cold
3. look
4. off
5. pretty
6. noisy
7. fly
8. sour
9. hard
10. shake